My Irish Dance Journal

Calendar Year

2nd Edition

An SFS Journal

ISBN: 1495379183
ISBN-13: 978-1495379185

DEDICATION

To my Father – Thank you for the many hours you spent, driving us to practice, to all the feiseanna, and for putting up with us in the car. To my Mother – I miss you always.

This Journal is also dedicated to you, the Irish Dancer, to your parents, grandparents, siblings, and all of your family members who are a part of your Irish Dance journey. May your journey be long, and full of adventure, excitement and success.

.

CONTENTS

ACKNOWLEDGMENTS

Thank you to Brennan Stidham for her insights into young dancers and their needs. Thank you to Patricia Silver, Ashley Middleton, and Charmaine Forbes for their support and insights.

My Irish Dance Journal

.

My Contract with Myself

I,_____, hereby agree and commit to take the following steps to improve my accountability to myself and to increase my chances for my competitive and personal Irish Dance success:

I will not let one small slip-up convince me that I'm stupid, worthless, or a lost cause. I will respect myself by refusing to engage in verbal self-abuse, and I will find positive ways to comfort and support myself when I'm having a hard time. Specifically, I will_____

_____

I will not sacrifice my practice time for non-productive pursuits, wasting time, making other people happy at my expense, or doing for them what they can and should be doing for themselves. When there is a conflict between my practice and dance plans and what other people want me to do, I will negotiate to find a reasonable solution that allows me to do what I need to do for myself. I will also ensure that my academic success remains a priority equal to or exceeding that of my Irish Dance aspirations.

I choose to be responsible for my decisions and behavior. I will ask myself what's most important to me at that moment and make my decision. If I don't like the consequences, I will try something different the next time.

I will, at all times, embody the qualities of self-confidence, self-esteem, healthy eating habits, academic achievement, school spirit, and community involvement, and will honor my position as a role model for younger dancers.

_____

My signature on the line indicates the seriousness with which I will approach my year's work toward improvement of my dancing ability.

All About Me!!

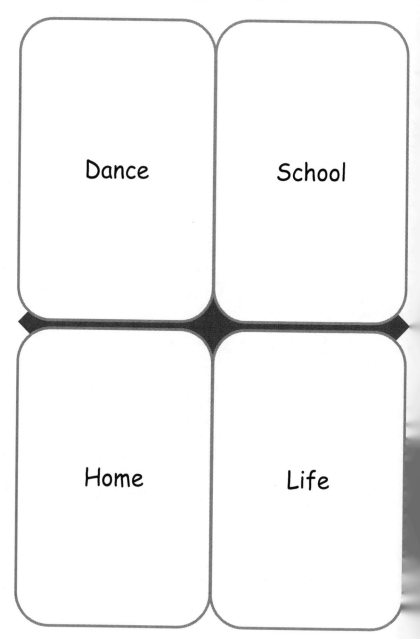

Dance

School

Home

Life

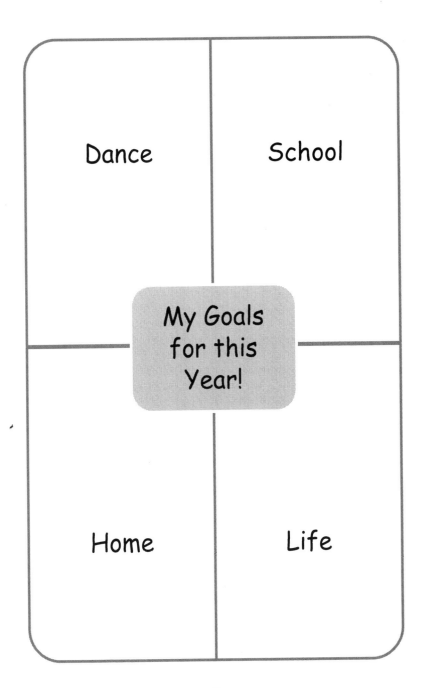

Dance

School

My Goals
for this
Year!

Home

Life

Dances: Know and Compete

Dance	Highest Level I Know	My Competition Level	My Goal Level for This Year
Reel			
Light Jig			
Single Jig			
Slip Jig			
Treble Jig			
Hornpipe			

Set Dances	Know	Compete
St. Patrick's Day		
The Blackbird		
Job of Journeywork		
The Garden of Daisies		

Act as if it were impossible to fail.
~ Dorothea Brande

You miss one hundred percent of the shots you don't take.
~ Wayne Gretzky

Dances: Know and Compete

Ceílí & Group Dances	Know	Compete
4-Hands		
6-Hands		
8-Hands		
Other		

 # JANUARY

Start of Month Grades in School:

Subject	Grade

My Goals for this Month:

1.	
2.	
3.	
4.	
5.	
6.	
7.	

Really Important Things to Remember:

1.	
2.	
3.	
4.	
5.	
6.	
7.	
8.	

You will never change your life until you change something you do daily. ~ Mike Murdoc

My Practice Log

Date	# of Minutes	Parent Signature

Irish Dance Class Notes

Date	Teacher Notes	Teacher Signature

Irish Dance Class Notes

Date	Teacher Notes	Teacher Signature

Monthly Time Sheet
(in minutes)

Date	Irish Dance	Home Work	Sports	Chores	My Initials
1					
2					
3					
4					
5					
6					
7					
8					
9					
10					
11					
12					
13					
14					
15					
16					
17					
18					
19					
20					
21					
22					
23					
24					
25					
26					
27					
28					
29					
30					
31					

Feis Journal, January

Feis:_____

Dance	Level	Result

Feis:_____

Dance	Level	Result

Feis:_____

Dance	Level	Result

 # FEBRUARY

Start of Month Grades in School:

Subject	Grade

My Goals for this Month:

1.	
2.	
3.	
4.	
5.	
6.	
7.	

Really Important Things to Remember:

1.	
2.	
3.	
4.	
5.	
6.	
7.	
8.	

On the mountains of truth you can never climb in vain;
either you will reach a point higher up today, or you will be
training your powers so that you will be able to climb
higher tomorrow. ~ Friedrich Nietzsche

My Practice Log

Date	# of Minutes	Parent Signature

Irish Dance Class Notes

Date	Teacher Notes	Teacher Signature

Irish Dance Class Notes

Date	Teacher Notes	Teacher Signature

Monthly Time Sheet
(in minutes)

Date	Irish Dance	Home Work	Sports	Chores	My Initials
1					
2					
3					
4					
5					
6					
7					
8					
9					
10					
11					
12					
13					
14					
15					
16					
17					
18					
19					
20					
21					
22					
23					
24					
25					
26					
27					
28					
29					

Feis Journal, February

Feis:_____

Dance	Level	Result

Feis:_____

Dance	Level	Result

Feis:_____

Dance	Level	Result

 # MARCH

Start of Month Grades in School:

Subject	Grade

My Goals for this Month:

1.	
2.	
3.	
4.	
5.	
6.	
7.	

Really Important Things to Remember:

1.	
2.	
3.	
4.	
5.	
6.	
7.	
8.	

We cannot solve our problems with the same thinking we used when we created them. ~Albert Einstein

My Practice Log

Date	# of Minutes	Parent Signature

Irish Dance Class Notes

Date	Teacher Notes	Teacher Signature

Irish Dance Class Notes

Date	Teacher Notes	Teacher Signature

Monthly Time Sheet
(in minutes)

Date	Irish Dance	Home Work	Sports	Chores	My Initials
1					
2					
3					
4					
5					
6					
7					
8					
9					
10					
11					
12					
13					
14					
15					
16					
17					
18					
19					
20					
21					
22					
23					
24					
25					
26					
27					
28					
29					
30					
31					

Feis Journal, March

Feis:_____

Dance	Level	Result

Feis:_____

Dance	Level	Result

Feis:_____

Dance	Level	Result

 # APRIL

Start of Month Grades in School:

Subject	Grade

My Goals for this Month:

1.	
2.	
3.	
4.	
5.	
6.	
7.	

Really Important Things to Remember:

1.	
2.	
3.	
4.	
5.	
6.	
7.	
8.	

In the confrontation between the stream and the rock, the stream always wins – not through strength but by perseverance. ~ H Jackson Browne

My Practice Log

Date	# of Minutes	Parent Signature

Irish Dance Class Notes

Date	Teacher Notes	Teacher Signature

Irish Dance Class Notes

Date	Teacher Notes	Teacher Signature

Monthly Time Sheet
(in minutes)

Date	Irish Dance	Home Work	Sports	Chores	My Initials
1					
2					
3					
4					
5					
6					
7					
8					
9					
10					
11					
12					
13					
14					
15					
16					
17					
18					
19					
20					
21					
22					
23					
24					
25					
26					
27					
28					
29					
30					

Feis Journal, April

Feis:_____

Dance	Level	Result

Feis:_____

Dance	Level	Result

Feis:_____

Dance	Level	Result

 # MAY

Start of Month Grades in School:

Subject	Grade

My Goals for this Month:

1.	
2.	
3.	
4.	
5.	
6.	
7.	

Really Important Things to Remember:

1.	
2.	
3.	
4.	
5.	
6.	
7.	
8.	

You gain strength, courage, and confidence by every
experience in which you really stop to look fear in the face.
You must do the thing which you think you cannot do.
~ Eleanor Roosevelt

My Practice Log

Date	# of Minutes	Parent Signature

Irish Dance Class Notes

Date	Teacher Notes	Teacher Signature

Irish Dance Class Notes

Date	Teacher Notes	Teacher Signature

Monthly Time Sheet
(in minutes)

Date	Irish Dance	Home Work	Sports	Chores	My Initials
1					
2					
3					
4					
5					
6					
7					
8					
9					
10					
11					
12					
13					
14					
15					
16					
17					
18					
19					
20					
21					
22					
23					
24					
25					
26					
27					
28					
29					
30					
31					

Feis Journal, May

Feis:_____

Dance	Level	Result

Feis:_____

Dance	Level	Result

Feis:_____

Dance	Level	Result

 JUNE

Start of Month Grades in School:

Subject	Grade

My Goals for this Month:

1.	
2.	
3.	
4.	
5.	
6.	
7.	

Really Important Things to Remember:

1.	
2.	
3.	
4.	
5.	
6.	
7.	
8.	

Your mind, while blessed with permanent memory, is cursed with lousy recall. Written goals provide clarity. By documenting your dreams, you must think about the process of achieving them. ~ Gary Ryan Blair

My Practice Log

Date	# of Minutes	Parent Signature

Irish Dance Class Notes

Date	Teacher Notes	Teacher Signature

Irish Dance Class Notes

Date	Teacher Notes	Teacher Signature

Monthly Time Sheet
(in minutes)

Date	Irish Dance	Home Work	Sports	Chores	My Initials
1					
2					
3					
4					
5					
6					
7					
8					
9					
10					
11					
12					
13					
14					
15					
16					
17					
18					
19					
20					
21					
22					
23					
24					
25					
26					
27					
28					
29					
30					

Feis Journal, June

Feis:_____

Dance	Level	Result

Feis:_____

Dance	Level	Result

Feis:_____

Dance	Level	Result

 # JULY

Start of Month Grades in School:

Subject	Grade

My Goals for this Month:

1.	
2.	
3.	
4.	
5.	
6.	
7.	

Really Important Things to Remember:

1.	
2.	
3.	
4.	
5.	
6.	
7.	
8.	

Don't ask yourself what the world needs; ask yourself what
makes you come alive. And then go and do that. Because
what the world needs is people who have come alive.
~ Howard Thurman

My Practice Log

Date	# of Minutes	Parent Signature

Irish Dance Class Notes

Date	Teacher Notes	Teacher Signature

Irish Dance Class Notes

Date	Teacher Notes	Teacher Signature

Monthly Time Sheet
(in minutes)

Date	Irish Dance	Home Work	Sports	Chores	My Initials
1					
2					
3					
4					
5					
6					
7					
8					
9					
10					
11					
12					
13					
14					
15					
16					
17					
18					
19					
20					
21					
22					
23					
24					
25					
26					
27					
28					
29					
30					
31					

Feis Journal, July

Feis:_____

Dance	Level	Result

Feis:_____

Dance	Level	Result

Feis:_____

Dance	Level	Result

AUGUST

Start of Month Grades in School:

Subject	Grade

My Goals for this Month:

1.	
2.	
3.	
4.	
5.	
6.	
7.	

Really Important Things to Remember:

1.	
2.	
3.	
4.	
5.	
6.	
7.	
8.	

Success is not a place at which one arrives, but rather the spirit with which one undertakes and continues the journey.   ~ Alex Nobel

My Practice Log

Date	# of Minutes	Parent Signature

Irish Dance Class Notes

Date	Teacher Notes	Teacher Signature

Irish Dance Class Notes

Date	Teacher Notes	Teacher Signature

Monthly Time Sheet
(in minutes)

Date	Irish Dance	Home Work	Sports	Chores	My Initials
1					
2					
3					
4					
5					
6					
7					
8					
9					
10					
11					
12					
13					
14					
15					
16					
17					
18					
19					
20					
21					
22					
23					
24					
25					
26					
27					
28					
29					
30					
31					

Feis Journal, August

Feis:_____

Dance	Level	Result

Feis:_____

Dance	Level	Result

Feis:_____

Dance	Level	Result

 # SEPTEMBER

Start of Month Grades in School:

Subject	Grade

My Goals for this Month:

1.	
2.	
3.	
4.	
5.	
6.	
7.	

Really Important Things to Remember:

1.	
2.	
3.	
4.	
5.	
6.	
7.	
8.	

Your time is limited, so don't waste it living someone else's life ~ Steve Jobs

My Practice Log

Date	# of Minutes	Parent Signature

Irish Dance Class Notes

Date	Teacher Notes	Teacher Signature

Irish Dance Class Notes

Date	Teacher Notes	Teacher Signature

Monthly Time Sheet
(in minutes)

Date	Irish Dance	Home Work	Sports	Chores	My Initials
1					
2					
3					
4					
5					
6					
7					
8					
9					
10					
11					
12					
13					
14					
15					
16					
17					
18					
19					
20					
21					
22					
23					
24					
25					
26					
27					
28					
29					
30					

Feis Journal, September

Feis:_____

Dance	Level	Result

Feis:_____

Dance	Level	Result

Feis:_____

Dance	Level	Result

 **OCTOBER**

Start of Month Grades in School:

Subject	Grade

My Goals for this Month:

1.	
2.	
3.	
4.	
5.	
6.	
7.	

Really Important Things to Remember:

1.	
2.	
3.	
4.	
5.	
6.	
7.	
8.	

You see things; and you say, 'Why?" But I dream things
that never were; and I say, "Why not?"
~ George Bernard Shaw

My Practice Log

Date	# of Minutes	Parent Signature

Irish Dance Class Notes

Date	Teacher Notes	Teacher Signature

Irish Dance Class Notes

Date	Teacher Notes	Teacher Signature

Monthly Time Sheet
(in minutes)

Date	Irish Dance	Home Work	Sports	Chores	My Initials
1					
2					
3					
4					
5					
6					
7					
8					
9					
10					
11					
12					
13					
14					
15					
16					
17					
18					
19					
20					
21					
22					
23					
24					
25					
26					
27					
28					
29					
30					
31					

Feis Journal, October

Feis:_____

Dance	Level	Result

Feis:_____

Dance	Level	Result

Feis:_____

Dance	Level	Result

NOVEMBER

Start of Month Grades in School:

Subject	Grade

My Goals for this Month:

1.	
2.	
3.	
4.	
5.	
6.	
7.	

Really Important Things to Remember:

1.	
2.	
3.	
4.	
5.	
6.	
7.	
8.	

At the center of your being you have the answer; you know who you are and you know what you want. ~ Lao Tzu

My Practice Log

Date	# of Minutes	Parent Signature

Irish Dance Class Notes

Date	Teacher Notes	Teacher Signature

Irish Dance Class Notes

Date	Teacher Notes	Teacher Signature

Monthly Time Sheet
(in minutes)

Date	Irish Dance	Home Work	Sports	Chores	My Initials
1					
2					
3					
4					
5					
6					
7					
8					
9					
10					
11					
12					
13					
14					
15					
16					
17					
18					
19					
20					
21					
22					
23					
24					
25					
26					
27					
28					
29					
30					

Feis Journal, November

Feis:_____

Dance	Level	Result

Feis:_____

Dance	Level	Result

Feis:_____

Dance	Level	Result

 # DECEMBER

Start of Month Grades in School:

Subject	Grade

My Goals for this Month:

1.	
2.	
3.	
4.	
5.	
6.	
7.	

Really Important Things to Remember:

1.	
2.	
3.	
4.	
5.	
6.	
7.	
8.	

You may be disappointed if you fail, but you are doomed if you don't try. ~ Beverly Sills

My Practice Log

Date	# of Minutes	Parent Signature

Irish Dance Class Notes

Date	Teacher Notes	Teacher Signature

Irish Dance Class Notes

Date	Teacher Notes	Teacher Signature

Monthly Time Sheet
(in minutes)

Date	Irish Dance	Home Work	Sports	Chores	My Initials
1					
2					
3					
4					
5					
6					
7					
8					
9					
10					
11					
12					
13					
14					
15					
16					
17					
18					
19					
20					
21					
22					
23					
24					
25					
26					
27					
28					
29					
30					
31					

Feis Journal, December

Feis:_____

Dance	Level	Result

Feis:_____

Dance	Level	Result

Feis:_____

Dance	Level	Result

End of Year Review

What I Accomplished This Year: _____

_____
_____
_____
_____
_____
_____

What Could Have Gone Better This Year: _____

_____
_____
_____
_____
_____
_____

Things I'm Proud of in My Life: _____

_____
_____
_____
_____
_____
_____

What I Want to Accomplish Next Year: _____

_____
_____
_____
_____
_____
_____

End of Year Review

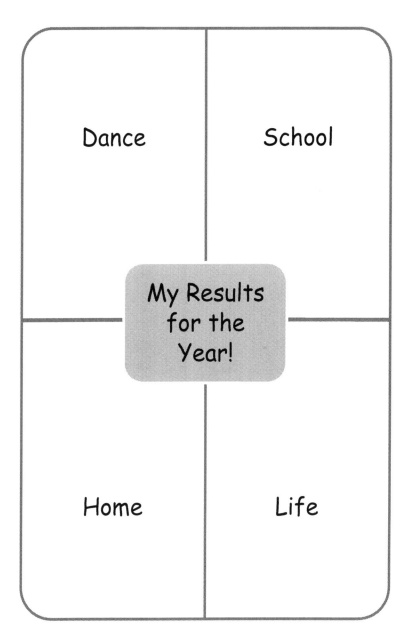

Dance

School

My Results for the Year!

Home

Life

Dances: Know and Compete

Dance	Highest Level I Know	My Competition Level	My Goal Level for Next Year
Reel			
Light Jig			
Single Jig			
Slip Jig			
Treble Jig			
Hornpipe			

Set Dances	Know	Compete
St. Patrick's Day		
The Blackbird		
Job of Journeywork		
The Garden of Daisies		

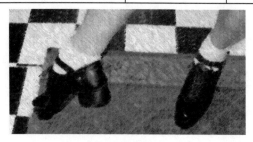

Dances: Know and Compete

Ceílí & Group Dances	Know	Compete
4-Hands		
6-Hands		
8-Hands		
Other		

ABOUT THE AUTHOR

A certified Irish Dance teacher and adjudicator, Sharon Flynn Stidham holds a Bachelor's degree in Mathematics and a Master's Degree in Business Administration. In addition to her Irish Dance pursuits, she is a College Professor, a certified Secondary teacher of Mathematics, and an artist. She began her studies in Irish Dance in 1969 with Joan McNiff Cass, TCRG/ADCRG, and continued with her brother, IDTANA co-founder, Cyril McNiff, TCRG/ADCRG (RIP). Her Open Champion dancing career was completed in her early twenties, but Irish Dance remained her dream, and she eventually completed her goals of achieving her TCRG and ADCRG, and of opening her own Irish Dance school. As a parent, she has spent years helping her own children track their many hours spent in dance practice, music practice, studying, homework, completing projects and writing papers. This journal is intended to make life easier for Irish Dance students around the world, tracking their accomplishments, their goals and their aspirations.

Made in the USA
San Bernardino, CA
10 December 2018